LOST CALLS

64 Poems

Kerry Brown

First Edition

Produced and Distributed By:

Library Partners Press

ZSR Library

Wake Forest University

1834 Wake Forest Road

Winston-Salem, North Carolina 27106

library partners press

a digital publishing imprint

www.librarypartnerspress.org

To Rebecca Hope

The author would like to express
his deep gratitude to
Amina Alya, Chu Shu, and Aimee Zheng
for their many helpful comments and
suggestions for this sequence.

About the Poems

This sequence of 64 short poems represent an inquiry on the theme of absence and the complex feelings and associated language and images it gives rise to.

Written between 2014 and 2015, partly in Australia, partly in the UK, and in Taiwan and Hong Kong, each one distils a moment in which affections and memories are reawakened towards a person, and places or experiences they are associated with.

They record the various ways in which absence in the life of someone present figures constantly as a source of struggle, disquiet, and tension, and figure ways in which this disruption is managed and, partially, pacified.

About the Cover

The cover shows a detail from the north wall of Minster Abbey in Sheppey, Kent, in the UK. This ancient wall contains fabric from Roman, Saxon and later periods. It provides a puzzle to observers because of the ways in which its texture and surface, with no easy logic, mixes up residues from these different eras, meshing them together across the surface of the wall.

--Kerry Brown

1

When I am seaside where
light breeze stirs stillness alive
heading up beside the north beech
lying by creeping suburbs, I pass away
trying to keep to my time.
The day's stray wind dispels
an encroaching memory
containing only you, and
at that moment something hurts
which I will to fade. This
is because of you? It hardly seems so.
More like because of me.
Keep to the tide: Beside the sea
never forget to remember

2

What do I mean when I say I am yours
and that we truly belong to each other?
Who are we with when we aren't together
bearing in mind this is all of the time?
Does this mean we love absence?
Is that the thing we seek to embrace?
Is solitude the preferred companion,
making up for what it unmakes?
I think of bright daylight, your shadow
crossing the room, going out to a park,
lingering by corners, pressing on your way.
I think of your form happy, till it dissolves
out of my control, escaping my clarity.
Emptying my soul's emptiness in your's.

3

Cumulus, cirrus, monochrome clouds
splashed with colour by a shaft of sun,
their shadows playing upon the earth
binding downwards on the vacant under space,
they carry with them the sense
of something like a memory of something
that feels like it never was. The many ways
I have made up to recompense myself
for the lack of you, of your presence
in memory, putting you where you are not.
I merely feign you, hope you into place
where figments are servants performing you,
taking the place that is rightfully yours,
in the zone of our non-meeting, ill lit
by light shed from imagined suns.

4

That the smudged sky's light dies in dusk
is irrefutable; that I daily talk to you
in my heart stands in the same truth.
That we converse across immovable boundaries –
that is unusual. But for us
a kind of normal, a kind of way
we have to do things. I remember corridors,
places for fleeing, green banks saturated
with floods of sinking sunshine.
And all these things are united
by the rise of anger at my missing
what promised you but never was,
admitting to myself I will never
be allowed to truly recollect you.

5

Late strorm; first dead night sky
cut alive by flash. My city's heart
is isolated, silenced, confounded.
Thunder's power is instinctive,
proves the way I create havens
in the day, realms of light, sure things to say,
because in the night storm there is little to say.
Slumbering when quietness comes again,
when sleep dies, I say: This will be the day
when I say something, have something to say
of the way I love, of love's rhythm ruling my life.
An encroaching black shape seals my hope's end,
someone who is not you speaks for you and says:
ache with the longing for her body never next to yours,
bury her memory in the storm, seeking what she defers.

6

Striving to live like your beauty is my life,
stating this truth from what I call my heart,
while my mind vows to resist, split apart
defiant only in the trapped moment, feeling this,
first I am walking along the ancient track
then flee over ground, knowing what I know,
trying to get to the next field
understanding there is hope there
which will be gone when I arrive.
So I see, say `the hill', say `the green bank'
`The fallen tree,' `the path', `grass'.
Echoes in this space grow long. Short stories lengthen,
long stories fail. Rise to the point to say it:
see these things, or there is nothing to see.

7

Was I wrong trying not to err?
Foolish for trying to be still? Someone
who liked searching for something
not believing it while it was true?
I sat on the hill, clouds moving crossway
eyes hunting horizons then falling away,
reaching to embrace, stretching my hands
and imagination empty, failing
then and there. The end of heaven
lies over the hill. There your still form
lies open to waking, but slumbering
beyond my ambition. A nuclear moment
of feeling, wanting, waiting, yearning,
for things that get me closer to escaping you.

8

Sun seen through storm clouds, on a flight
nearly aborted. Heaven's release
of tension in electric waves. Through oval window
sight of a slash of momentary light, stabbing down
till extinguished in grey dead earth.
I am here. You where, no one knows
solid as airy, angel soul.
In the graveyard ten thousand miles away
when we knew where we were, we paused in early night,
only the shadow marked division between us.
I calculated, summed up wrong, did nothing
which was right. Walked back and talked of love
through poems. Stood uncomfortably still
then stirred, losing the moment briefly there
like the flashes which had lived and died in air

9

Morsels of meaning. Sentences shrinking, melting
down to phrases, phrases down to words,
words standing alone then sinking
to a silence that is continuing
and how do I respond? Words of my own
said to me and no one? Investment with no return.
I venture out, find the place I desire
trying to catch yours falling on someone's ears
stealing what was unmeant for me.
It rained constantly in Canada. A deserted hotel.
I did not leave my room. Wrote and fretted
and then sent those words, like emissaries
doomed by the hope of their task.

10

After your first death in my life
your words died with you. I was bereft
and on my own wrote endlessly, hoping this
would shore against my fractiousness.
In the time of my fragmentation
not blood but my words poured from me
born from the wound, pain's recompense.
On your resurrection into my life,
I used those old words to greet your return.
I do not mourn the expense
of the words that died to save my mind
and brought me from desiring death.
Their sacrifice alone resisted demise:
Words heal words' wounding distress.

11

Boundless white stretched across all sight
and seeing nothing, except for something
on the expanse to the right – a blemish
marking an area torn deep, threading through
to another side. Closed eyes observing this
-mine- then hurting, naked, open under the one sun.
Sabbath. A day of staring and waiting.
Sun dies and then rain beats on bare roofs.
Drum sound. Think. Presentiment of a life to come
away from all of this, where light and shadows
are mixed into one. A world where living
means something different, time goes somewhere else,
where someone somehow comes along,
when I dream of being more than me and mean
a me that could be real by being with you.

12

Stones jumbled, mixed, in this one wall,
granite, diorite, horsfels, markfeldite,
and local limestone, sandstone, exotic or demotic
with colours from pale to scorched brown or black,
residue from the ancient fire attacks.
All of this open behind you, in the southern wall,
a symphony of stone types from the old realm
made into a single surface of composite elements.
You smile back, a dim day, into the camera;
holding a coat to you. A kind light ray
but merely a suggestion, nothing overt.
The closed door of the great church
with its beast carved on the wall, stone arms raised
haunts your left side.
Brixworth. Mid UK. April or early May.

13

But before all this, in the church of varied stone
there had been another time. Good Friday, made sombre
by tears the night before on the way
weeping in a roadside hotel, taking the holiday
trafficless road to the place on the map the next day
obedient to the mark where the great church stands.
We were together inside before the blackened altar
less Jesus for the day his death was signified
then retreating shadows on the ground. Your footfalls.
Your voice saying you were going out.
Fear when I was alone, standing by the arch,
exiting myself to the dull midday. Appalled
I did not want you, you were not there,
felled by the edge of the twisted stair.

14

April, English time, she comes and wills
clarity about what we both are, demands
answers neither can yet give, leaves a memory
of suffering. May she is absent largely
back to her own land. Her face
is present only through words she has left,
images driven to the back of my mind
emerge from repression, drifting again
into conscious light. June she stands
ready to re-engage. Winning the lost time
now uppermost. By July it is near night,
in my time her energy lies low again.
Hovering nearby beside my past
actress assuming all emotions bar one – love.

15

Lord! The fresh air betokens
the solitude I thought, and one
stands by the end of the long field
surrendered to its vast green heart.
It is on this day I take refuge
from any bitter renunciation
hiding myself in the half grown crop
that suggests an implicit philosophy
through its inchoate form, its shape.
I walk in this space to verify; I seek terms
in the boundaries of this thing
that existed in some way
before the lord of the moment
set it before me on this passing day.

16

I had made the promise to be with you
and booked the ticket. And then silence
came from your end. Her dying was unavoidable
and nothing came from you. Both brought fear.
She was tired living, held out till deep winter
and every day I could I came and sat
and watched, doing nothing except seeing
some one else become no-one again.
I was in the hall in the hospital
before she finally left. No breath
and a frozen look when I came in
to a place that was, after all
properly sterile. I can handle her finished face, fixed;
yours is harder, not present, never mine.

17

The illness of searching was the cause of it;
the restless need to sit once you had gone
where you had sat, in the haunted place
in the village pub, beside the church, and calculate
abstractly, on the surface of the table there
the various components of my used up self
that now could be disposed of.
Head. Heart. Stomach. Veins. Blood.
A brutal sum that took the better part of noon
till it was done. I went on my way
reconfigured, holding to the path, fought.
I was ready for the bowed trees upsetting sun.
Shadow way. A place where nettles bite bare flesh
beside which I stood, undone by cruelly naked green.

18

Desiring absence after the smashed night
following turbulence when the shouting started
the atmosphere from the TV became irrelevant
when the duet of screams kicked off
finding no resolution till the thrown glass
hit the wall. The remorse of going
was better than regretting to stay.
Removal is a part of love, a fraction of its ritual.
Togetherness of the wrong kind is poison. Closed
hands tangle, anger breaks
energy disintegrates, and after that
no place but go away only ever to restart.

19

Is the kiss alone, sitting at the edge
meaningful if it is set apart
from all the other things around it –
The excitement of first meeting after so long
the long sentences, the words, catching up
the strong conversing, drinking
and the food. Is it permissible
to lift this out? The second lips touched,
before an awkward pause, then the further venture in.
Put this simply, these actions stand alone
and things alone can be discounted.
Can I ever, by myself, bind it to something, bring it in,
encompass it, in a skein of meaning
aware of the other's non-assent?

20

Better to see that moment as one of execution,

not affirming intimacy, or vindicating hints before.

A delusive time before the brittle wake up,

when truth fell from a cloud-free sky.

Before, I was free of sentiments

and then the images came with their entrapment

of soft lips together, tongues pushing together,

hands squeezed. A solemn walk after all of this

holding each other, inadequately, to stand still in shadows

by the subway exit. Exhilaration this proved something

proved still born. In dawn light alone I knew

when I stood nakedly before the mirror

I was holding an image of something already dead,

her exiting everywhere except my memory.

21

I am eating in the limpid light. The day
is half over; so far I have surrendered nothing,
said goodbye to no one. Simply desire being still
to hear enough of the rhythms of my heart
and the sound of the world I am surrounded by, an island
of internal noises, audible only to myself.
I am aware of the tug, the pull, the lure
Of sensation, of being plugged in
to greater spectacle. I am aware of someone
who means nothing to me wandering close by
and in a glance across to me – a dart of their eye
they capture something involuntarily
that transfers the memory of the sense of you
and I fight to find my peace again.

22

Deep night, and the soft deadly bed
is the place where I struggle with myself
and another who was banned from there. Silent spirit
links through no time and no space
bearing a loyalty unknown to any other.
Promises of feeling finally unsaid, even in the recess
of my inner lying heart. I am speaking
as my place shrinks, trekking towards a door
opening inwards, the dimensions garbled,
mixed to confuse me. Pronouns are a hindrance -
you, he, I – we are all helpless, undefended.
Invading logic makes the move in.
Answer: Seek the most vulnerable course:
seize the ideal of her. Win distraction.

23

How sweet the sunshine passing, intense, dry,
with you heavily nice, variously other,
beside me in the arbour .Afterwards still till dawn
when all the makeshift gestures of intimacy start up–
words tumbling upwards where we lie.
A cathedral air in your sounds, a busy chorale
in the grand facade that limits the way
towards true inwardness. I reseek
the threads of thought back to you. Reaffirm,
letting the sweet time pass and when past
reigniting their first sense. In my waste
I see puddled dirt, tears, the race
to get out, to be released from thick passion,
weary of the way this always ends my freedom.

24

Now the problem: the voice I speak is always there
seeking its natural outlet through words, rising,
a purity in its tone, rhythmic as it searches
the pace of each word's best sound. Then
this imperative for the meant infects intonation.
I seek ways to try to capture how to say the woe
I feel at the unconnectivity of this my self to others.
Now I seek to heal the split; I aim to throw my voice forward
as an act of recovery, letting it, singing, hand back to me
the completion of desired meaning. Revelation for today:
The meant is not in the words but in the way they try to say,
that at least means beyond the poor reach of a word's meaning
And tone of all the things I had said this day is unsparing.
Brute statement of blame: wanting you, and in the want failing

25

My spirit linked to someone out of sight,
purely irresolute. Nagging quandaries
in the dark noon, when rain from clouds
half heartedly divides the soft air.
Taking refuge under border trees. There
she waits for me, a shadow, whispering,
attentive to my unease, and to the toil
of this placeless love. A breeze picks up
the end of questions, stirs residual leaves
from another season. I am ensnared
in this heavy atmosphere. A stark birdcall
shrill, awakens instinct. A warning:
Fear the first step into the wood. Then step.

26

From the outside its surfaces look placid:
lake in a sunny place, a pathway by the edge,
a man in a black suit, treading, arriving
at the cafe terrace. Bowing and kissing
an acquaintance there. Orders food,
swamped in delicate meandering
conversation. And maybe one of them
is thinking of their fear of death, of the end
of things, or of the destruction of what matters.
and the other, do they know anything of this?
Exercised by this rule of distance, by the hour
when the sighing lover takes their leave,
but leaves their self in the other's mind.
An ice cream melts in someone else's hand.

27

I am sun-bright, at ease, the recent tension
all relieved, holding her words written tangibly
in a yellow-paged letter, sent after the Paris debacle
when she had felled me unambiguously.
Nothing personal, she said, just was the way things were.
But I refuse to accept, preferring to be cruel to myself.
At the edge of the college cathedral green
staring out over darkening late autumn fields
a rural idyll in the city centre
with its sterility, all is humming and silence.
The background sound of Cambridge, presenting
at least one diversion. Dusk, upswing of heart,
lending me a moment of tense relief
before the return of renewed old grief.

28

I progress into this false start,
propounding fact as we move forward
over the tiles of the ground floor, peering
into the museum chamber, voices hushed,
faced with a bigger meaning, sharper sentiments
as the doors close behind us. And we go down
narrow steps, to the sarcophagus,
sitting restlessly among concreted walls,
our hands playing along its cold edges
ignoring whatever sense of death we get there.
A sharp moment. The one incidence of joint reality
breaking at a point where we re-step up
rising to ground level once more. Ignore what's said.
Seek for something live; leave the already dead.

29

You are mine for this moment at least, in my vision,

but not mine, because of how your eyes search

far away from me. Mine as we walk together

and our words intermingle. But really not mine

as you veer to your life and I veer to mine.

After your departure, you become fearsome,

someone I could not think about, a person

transformed into something spectral.

I dreamed of you when you had gone,

living with a reality truer

than what you had with me.

A power looking into my eyes

pressing upon my conscious self,

making me wake from what was real.

30

A place, seeming quiet as I move through,
opening the gate, brushed by leaves, going
down in the left dip where the Roman road
is lying dusty, cleared of mud, nettles breaching
its frayed edge. This is the king's border,
this the place where the divided realm
had deeds violated by rattled men,
till their lords stilled their contending wills
and punishment fell. Generations on,
I am today fooled by the silence of this place.
Here is where I paused before the onset of clarity.
here is where I bowed my head in settlement,
here I decided on a path, relinquishing
the sentiments of this lying land's bequest.

31

What was achieved was not realised

What was said was not meant

What was known was not comprehended

What was owned was not possessed

What was hoped for was not aspired to

What was hurtful did not bring pain

What finished had never started

What delighted never happened,

at least with any joyousness.

Known from the start: Love is a problem

that needs to be resolved,

each of its word stalked by regret,

kidnapped by hope, anger, pain.

futile abundance with no gain.

32

Our times are different. Wondering about you
in weeks, I feel for you over days,
eeking out each word and gesture you have given
from seconds to fill an hour. Months pass
and still there is nothing. Then the truth:
The few words at the start were the only thing
of yours I will own. No actions. No things.
a benighted moment, mature with recognition:
our times belong to different realms
they will never hold together, embrace.
In my time, your image traps then flees.
In your time, I fade before I am.
You have nothing of me to disown:
My time is yours. Your time is your own.

33

Searching to know its age, the wall
is anciently inexplicable. North side by estuary,
a monastic church once, but the marks that scar it
are feeble clues. Nothing it offers to sight gives certainty
about when it began. Studying the explanation
from a book, looking up, interpreting
the poor remnants, I become you
a moment of exquisite balance, the zones
around the self fade, and we unite
in the holy silence of midday.
Defined moment, properly reverenced,
then sullied by abandonment.
Hunt again the scrambled map of age on the wall,
wondering why I seek dilapidation with you.

34

Tudely. In English green, a low brown brick church,
and inside, the blue washed into stained windows
into which our perceiving eyes swim. There is a cry
in this glass. A raw yellow colour hard
against the flood that stole her away
and made her family seek legacy in this bequest
of aquatic surface, murdered and then redeemed.
Along the road, up from the wooden gate
there is a stray, shaded wood path to left,
at least as I remember this. Recollection of the blue
fades here. But the cries are shrill and clear
coming through the colour, of that sinking girl,
fleeing down to her end in the water before ours.

35

You do nothing. Say nothing. Are nothing.
Cavernous, silent still. An empty form
with weight. A mighty nullity pressing down
on the spirit world which you claim to belong to
but never did. Your invisibility
is the source of all you are. A trick so old
it needs no reinvention. You stand still
and cause me to move to where I think you are.
But of course, there is not even a trace
of what you never left, because you never were,
still seeking you though you never moved
from where you were not to where you never are.

36

Orison light. Strong wind on the closed road.

Walking forward nowhere for no reason.Sole body

in touch, interlinked, with everyone, everything.

To myself: `If we never chose this life, we chose the way to live,

chose (or not) to live fully, not at the edge.

In it, not outside.' Pause. Again:`Love is embracing separation,

power exercised through distance, extending emotion

across the stellar spaces, from the solid enigma of `I'

to the places where `you' are anchored, present.'

Alone with myself all alone on my own,

In myself, now, and no place else.

Always seeking to say in silence what is unutterable.

Rocky hill and these lonely abandoned places

where I come, as I am, to be me for myself.

37

I saw you on the beach today
saying nothing. Nothing I had to say
would make you speak. So I was forced to say
words which entered the story, getting nothing back.
You were clear there, smiling, on the sand
face looking back. Your trousers lowered
over you bikini, the glimpse of flesh
was the sole speaking thing. Your eyes were empty.
You said, to me: I won't speak about anything,
it is all dead what was said before.
The only thing I can claim is what I now unsay.
And with your hand brushing against your skin
I dreamed you away, except your unsaid words,
pleading for them to stay while you had gone.

38

Nothing spoken, saying nothing again
saying it the same way. All I hear
is that the words don't come. Not coming
they always fail. Going to the shop, walking
on silent sunny dried tarmac. Tear myself from
death, the old lady falling. Nothing came
when she was weeping. Nothing lay inside
in the front room where the bed was moved.
There beside her, returned from my walk
I waited for your words, but they never came.
It was the same, long after the death.
Rain came. Snow fell. Still, from you, no words.

39

Thanking you for nothing,

rays with love fall from heaven

on the sparking pool. A head submerged,

baptised in the midday-heated water

smashing the tranquil image of a minute before

of the resplendent sun, of its imperium.

The sky god is obscured by storm clouds.

Threatening, but doing nothing. In my refuge,

far behind the eyes, I flee recall, avoid retrospect,

mind only the moment, the minute

I am in. Pace quickens. Upscale.

Seat myself before the source of control.

For a moment there is something.

Then you come and I abandon it.

40

Sky, and his high face, the Master
receding from his room. A knocked door
unanswered. And in the regret, the Master
glimpsed, swimming from view, suited,
before benighted me. I am speaking now
trying to restore myself to his favour
but he has collapsed from material life,
fallen away again from the status
I had surrendered to him. My Lord!
Take the sacrifice of my arrogance
as best recompense. Nothing I can give
can be better that what I gained
when I was denied by you.
Sweet rejection, set me free,
knowing now the debt is nullity.

41

Roads blocked. I seek termination
under another sky. June falls
and early night I stalk the answer
across town, in the bedroom she had fled to
summoned by her across the city
I ended up ending by her door, and the
slight ruffle, small shock, a crack
wholly open. She is there
clasped fully, a reality,
a stark stare, and her lover
spread on the bed, standing, fleeing.
Trust that never existed was never forfeited.
She bargained well on the small green
by the swelling traffic. Ill seen,
I conceded. We three were freed.

42

For her youth times were delightful,
serendipity not just sighted in shops
but a real thing. A close held course.
This writing, the Master said, will make you sane
teach you to reach the right spot
to keep the balance between logic and pain
to hold your emotion on a level edge
and in the interim before collapse
be granted sight, full understanding's gift.
I am sore with contemplation all this while,
caught in a hot spot. Booking revelation online
unperturbed by its late offering.
seek sunshine, seeing it so, so good
missing nothing of the world I never trod.

43

Me drowned, fractured, my latent wisdom
was concealed by the walls of sun
lit brick and the rectory by the closed church
where I took the route of familial burial
drowsy, by the path end, then across grass.
I lay, and search up to the writhing
clouds, the ungrammatical sky,
closed heavens. I could fall well,
never stop, reach light sources
out from my deserted body
deserving oblivion. I shut the light,
close my eyes and the wind breathes
light and meaningless across my face,
stirs her ways, her vagaries. Love leaves.

44

Desired comfort now rejected, its place
supplanted. Still falling rain, sobbing
on the sidewalk. I know this dying atmosphere
will never be regained. I stall,
nail its memory before it fades away.
Master, you told me in the upstairs room
to do this one thing: seek the meaning
before life, not after it. It sounded like a promise.
My mind is cleaned by the falling water.
I use it to finally answer back. I did try
but never dared to think at first
that everyone I needed there at the start
would vanish, with the meaning, in the finish.

45

The moment is all there is. A quiet place
by the doorway, in high summer. England
after the storm ended. The trouble
of her long departure, or her torn away
after a year of half surrendering.
She had pulled me into two that day
when we were here together then.
But I am in a calm space, sitting on a wood chair
just by the old stone door
and no one will come, which is welcome,
not here. No one will take this way,
sweet bliss, a pause, a slow moment
as the intensely real recedes
and I am prepared to be `I' again.

46

I grieved your loss, and grieved the time I spent
knowing nothing of you. Time consumed
with errant speculation which misled
the natural pace of life I wanted settled.
Double grieving, I only duplicated
by regretting the two griefs and how
they had appeared. A morning walk
with no sleep or purpose. The view
from the gentle hill of a field down
to the concealed river. Bird call stalled,
a hush, unearthly, like I had left
this place I already was in. Serene, pure,
the gap widening between thick clouds,
rising light falling away from where I was.

47

The shame was felt in a corner of room
slightly shaded by the oblique window
to the side of the attic, the house on a hill
and only brief sun, when there was day.
And there he, my former I, crept
and there he lifted himself from chains
of the daily burying – imagined, allowed himself
to be distracted for at least one moment
holding the image he most desired
in his closed eye. Do not attend ever
to the detail of the desire. Keep reality
when it is hurtful blurred. With people
do not figure in their eyes. Disappear
with your desire the moment it intensifies
or corrode with its burnt residue.

48

Happy with her, happy not, happy always
it was over, briefly, happy at the start
and then happy, but not knowing it
till the misery set in. The contrast
was an education, taking away the worn calm
of the early day. Downcast at midday
I struggled with my soul, sat in a coffee shop
going through the motions. Fought hard
and emerged in early afternoon, two lattes inside
before burial at midnight ended nightmare day.
The wolf crying, the teeth sharpened,
slaughtering my plated steak, unborn
to the moment when, thirst slated,
happiness emerged, and I lay low again.

49

I am room-enclosed, eyes wandering, filling
space with sweetness. A girl's breath
which is yours, sense of your glance
in deep uncertainty asking only me:
`Do you handle yourself well?'
(Do you put your mind in the right place)
`Have you obeyed the necessary edicts?'
(Forbidden thorough worship of yourself)
Made argumentative by the free day
my eyes demand what my heart prevents.
Against better objections my soul reneges.
A bitter struggle ending with failed defence.
She: Because you did not faithfully obey the game
Me: Because I never knew I was playing it.

50

May the lord of small returns, enraptured,
cast a line that captures a pure space
breaking it up into inner and outer. May joy
speak from the pages worked on. May reality
be ignored and its burden surrendered at the door
into happiness. Teeth tease the food,
feet spill across the floor. A dancing night.
Might we be pardoned for our evasion.
No need to pray, just evict ourselves
from the world of output construction.
Sit up. Sulk by the door. Be aware of deposits
and their inevitable inflation. How heart
is this place of happy submission.
May all this last as long as it has to, no longer.

51

I am scared the Lord's day will be sullied
by this worry of phoning through, of the dial,
the click of sound from elsewhere, an abused mobile,
trying to capture attention so clearly distracted
and loving the hateful thought of it:
Of her lying with her teeth open,
and her mouth formed into a gazing smile.
her head on the bed sheet and lovers
surrounding her, impounding this moment
grabbing it selfishly from my projected gaze.
My mouth is all of their mouths,
my distress a complaint against them.
My protests muffled by their buried ears
as I goad them to annihilating their desires.
This in service of my Sunday need.

52

Loving you, knowing the weight of that,
desiring nothing, not even to be free,
mistakenly taking the path away
to the place where I once more can't be.
Being in this state, solely aware of it
shackled to my time, ditched by it, rich
in its power to impede me. Smitten,
I am clown, a dullard, poor arse.
These are the labels you have fixed to me
all deserved. Without being these
what, I insist, would I be?
Tossed to a track already determined
losing myself before I find again
the feelings of your meaning to me.

53

Sea still, flotsam moveless. Winter sun on bay
edging towards horizon. Night imminent
and the sole mention of breeze on a dying wind.
Looking to the air, seeking it through
this still moment is unending. Dead present
commemorated at each moment that is past.
I am solid in this place, self apart
safe from the vagaries of emotion
that swirls and moves and seeks action,
seeks part of a world of fury and discomfort.
Gulls with gullets interrupt with calls.
Seaside and the lapping waves draw away
still I am recalled, back to the day
and memory fills the emptiness with plenitude.

54

Walking up to the field edge from hill place,
she is immovable, adamant, steady
in her rejection. It is a soft pause
before she steers to the path, ending
by seeking a barrier, staying there
and on the stile by wood, half smiling
she spells out my failures.
This is what you did not do, this was unsaid,
that was your first fall, and this the next.
Treading on brown and squelching earth
her feet do no wrong, and even as I seek
she is gone, illusive, along a long road
her feelings were intact, as nothing can be,
mine were in tatters, accountable to the failure
of thinking she had been where she was.

55

I wonder at how I became ill-blessed,

gifted to certainty I might never know you

finding cracks of hope in my doubts. I make up times

when I was with you, beside you, seeking entry in.

I was not barred. Indifference is weak

nothing to push back on. Extinct as vapid air

allowing `you' to be someone, but not mattering.

I seek flaws in my self-knowledge. Evasion.

Scatter my harsh certainty before hope clatters in.

You could do something but do nothing.

Somewhere you are doing something for someone,

but not for me, for whom you do nothing,

No thing of mine can breach your solitude.

Resisting knowledge solely by me of you.

56

Fitted here, a stair to righteousness –
Trouble, as eyes ill inhabited scramble,
seeking excuses to pause imagination.
Intense with barely teenage yearning,
I am atop in the attic, always doubtful
on the journey up. A window west
to the field aisles. Winterheld ice
on muddy ditch pools glistens from afar,
and hope back then this was part of a pattern
making towards a path, an end,
the glory of conquering desire,
of getting it right. In the night mother screams,
me undeceived, looking backwards,
doubtful, sober, looking at me to be, faltering, over.

57

Our anger would be better. Distaste
or contempt foreclosing strong dislike
spoken testament to rising antipathy
or some evidence of base intent.
`You're such an areshole'. That would work.
Or `You are divine', putting it another way.
But silence in unanswerable.
I can send my plaints in, decrees,
declarations, words, and they will pile
sky high, met with `access denied'.
The seed of destruction in their start,
inked in futility, terms stillborn, dead.
Words dole out finite misery,
silence is savage, aborting sense eternally.

58

Wanting to be in one piece, unwillingly unpicked,
discarding those loving selves that made me,
driven from that single life by wanting you to want me,
selves shedding skins, leaving traces, you unplacated.
The end is the start: throwing out my old self,
forging a new one that can be loved, but this one
meaning nothing to you too. Many times.
this me I have created to be liked by you
dies through the act he played a part in.
failed fulfilment is his demise. Changed,
he still doesn't reach you, still couldn't have you.
Coming back to my old self, I have moved on,
Reduced to less by trying to be more. All
chaos you never ordered, but which you directed.

59

Whore demanding the whole life of me
leering, and through a thick smile
peeling off the sleeves around my self.
Growing sick with the power of her radiant smile
counting the cost of it, discounting, I kiss in,
kiss the soft divisions, the skin, the pure
seamless patch between her breasts
and her stomach, down. Hungry, I demur
loving the way others love her, hating that too,
wanting them there beside me, against me,
as I forge against her, plough questions in
in wonder at the crowded life with her
and how they come when I am gone,
soul busy with day dreams of cuckoldry.

60

Winter. Alone watching the sails out at sea
pushed by wind to the disaster sands
west of the spot of mythical arrival
in antiquity. Deal beach in two times. A memory
of standing together in summer by the shrine
of a woman murdered centuries before
and in this stone alone remembered, both moved.
surrendering through this to another season.
The sharp wind remarries yesterday's moment
to the day today where I am here again. Exposed,
forlorn, on my own again, mood sinks in sea deep.
The year's end is like every ending I have known.
Dull to the bone, cold. Startled birds rise
and, wise or not, fly, fleet, to grey open sea.

61

It is just a tree, its branches long,

and when they reach into wind, they stir

in me a different longing, meaning more

than what the tree is. Its deep green

thrills and conceals and raises questions

in the winter day about the past when it grew here

and how it moves me from the moment it is in.

In spite of all the lack of stillness

in its thousand leaves, its agitation

when breeze falls into it, it does no wrong -

no shades of violence in the way it forever changes,

This thing that is much more than it is

For me becoming more than I am

when my sight and feelings marry with it.

62

Eternity lies at the base of things
underneath them. Pauses which extend
neverendingly, not intended at the start,
a failure to end that is limitless
until its limits ends, at the paramount moment
when things cease. No restart.
I seek peace with this malaise,
its heavy hand in every time in every thing:
on time when light bled through panes
onto a young world. On time when words
came tumbling out, before they fell back in
like expelled bandits gone to their home earth.
Face it hopelessly. You always were, will always be,
will live forever, and forever cease in me.

63

Gaze along the eyeline edge to where the green starts
keep the sight in sight of blue edging to nullity.
Still sky, still, and let wind arrive to depart,
let the sound of air all around everywhere
be sovereign. Be a part of all the things in sight
standing prime amongst their freed perspectives
but also alone, at their heart, seeing, meriting
the play of their forms across the scheme
of a world unfolding joyously for all to see
only now from this place. Remove solemnly,
place the park to west left, righteously
take from this rich world's plenitude
gifted from its heart to heart moved by wood,
trees, fields, and bounteous sky, loving solemnly till
dark.

64

To the mouth behind my teeth I leave
the saying of your name. The same each time
as words form, but different, moved on
in mood and sentiment. Each ventured according
to a new map of my failing feeling,
failed in the route to seek you,
arrive at your space. In this territory
my eyes send out voyagers, my instincts
are ill-soldiering. Dropping to the low defence
I let go of a thousand more words to do
what the thousand before did not do
but they are ill fated, ill disposed too,
and meet the wrath of your watchfulness
so praying in hope to end your indifference
    Is my soul defense.

About the Author

Kerry Brown is Professor of Chinese Studies and Director at the Lau China Institute at King's College, London.

This is his first book of poetry.

51289312R00047

Made in the USA
Charleston, SC
19 January 2016